Chants & Lamentations

By William Bay

Preface

This book contains seventeen lyrical, contemplative guitar solos appropriate for worship or concert settings. I have always been fond of Gregorian chants. Their simple yet pure melodies lend themselves to a wonderful freedom of expression and harmonic adaptation. Three of the chants are original and I included "Litany", a personal favorite from my book *Solo Guitar in Worship*.

I have also found that some of the most poignant Biblical texts are the lamentations. The soulful themes lend themselves to a myriad of individual expressions. Seven of the lamentations are original and all fall into the minor keys of Am, Dm, Em and Bm. Dropped-D tuning is used on the D minor solos. I find these pieces to be appropriate for Lent and Advent and also can be meaningful during communion services. I hope you enjoy performing these arrangements and compositions.

William Bay

Contents

Veni Creator 6

O God, Our Redeemer 8

Of the Father's Love Begotten 10

Ah, Holy Jesus 12

Veni redemptor gentium 14

I Look Unto the Hills 16

Litany 18

O Come, O Come, Emmanuel 20

Adoro Devote 22

Lamentation One 24

Lamentation Two 26

Lamentation Three 28

Lamentation Four 30

Lamentation Five 32

Lamentation Six 34

Lamentation Seven 36

Lamentation Eight 38

Chants

Veni Creator
O Come, Creator Spirit

O God, Our Redeemer

Freely

William Bay

Of the Father's Love Begotten
Divinum Mysterium

Ah, Holy Jesus
Ecce Jam Noctis

Freely

William Bay

C
17
21
21
25
25

Veni redemptor gentium
Come, Redeemer of the nations

12th Century Plainsong
William Bay

Gently

C

I Look Unto the Hills
From Whence Cometh My Help
Ps. 121:1

William Bay

16

Litany

With motion
C
a tempo
D
19

O Come, O Come, Emmanuel

Veni Emmanuel

Gently

9th Century Latin

20

24
D
29
34
39
21

Adoro Devote

Dropped-D Tuning

Moderately Slow

13th Century Plainsong

Guitar

Lamentations

Lamentation One

C

Lamentation Two

Lamentation Three

28

Lamentation Four

Moderately

William Bay

Lamentation Five

Lyrically

William Bay

Lamentation Six

Dropped-D Tuning

Freely

Wiliam Bay

34

Lamentation Seven

Flowing Tempo

William Bay

Lamentation Eight
Broad is the Road that Leads to Death

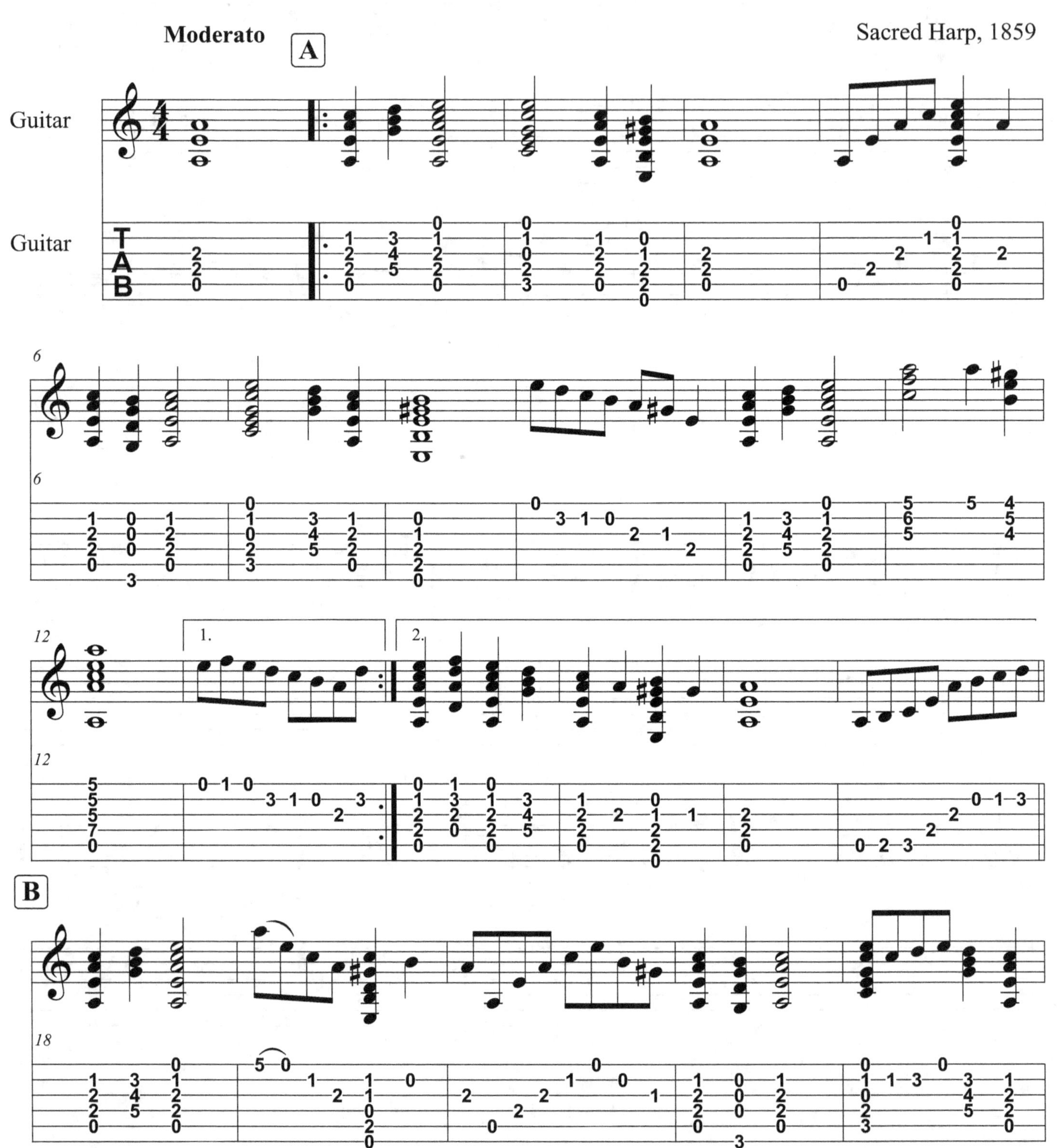

Other William Bay Sacred Guitar Books

Psalms for Guitar

Solo Guitar in Worship

Spirituals

Sacred Songs of Early America

Celtic Hymns and Sacred Songs

Lyrical Gospel Guitar Solos

Songs of Faith

Timeless Gospel Melodies

Country Gospel Guitar Solos

Christmas in the British Isles

An Early American Christmas

Sacred Guitar Solo Anthology

Sacred Guitar Solo Anthology #2

Beautiful Carols of Christmas

Hymns of Beauty and Strength

Gospel Guitar Encyclopedia

Communion

Devotion

100 Hymns for Trumpet & Guitar

100 Hymns for Flute & Guitar

100 Hymns for Violin & Guitars

100 Gospel Songs and Hymns for Trumpet & Guitar

100 Gospel Songs and Hymns for Flute & Guitar

100 Christmas Carols & Hymns for Trumpet & Guitar

100 Christmas Carols & Hymns for Flute & Guitar

WWW.MELBAY.COM